Digital India

The Exponential Growth

Contents

Preface

Twenty-three years ago, in June 1991, India had less than $1 billion in forex reserves, just sufficient to meet import requirements for three weeks. The government pledged 67 tonnes of Gold as collateral security to the International Monetary Fund to secure an emergency loan of $2.2 billion. Today, India is the fifth largest economy in the world, with a GDP of $3.7 trillion and a foreign reserve of $648.56 billion.

Once among the most unbanked countries in the world, today, India has become the most banked country. Now, India is the third largest digitalized country in the world, just behind the United States of America (USA) and China. India is in the number one position in terms of digital payments. As per the Reserve Bank of India (RBI), India's core digital economy has increased from 8.5% of GVA (Gross Value added-Economic productivity metric) in 2019 to 12.5% in 2023. In July 2015, the Indian government launched the Digital India program with the vision of changing India into a digitally empowered society. Through this program, the government is digitalizing all records, which is expected to reduce fraud.

To write this book, I got inspiration from Sir Nandan Nilekani's presentation on "India's Digital Transformation," available on YouTube by Business Today (BtTV). In His 30-plus minute in-depth talk, Nandan sir explains why India's digital growth is irreversible and nonlinear. Nothing happened for years in India; and then suddenly, something happens, and it just takes over. Even though I tend to disagree that nothing happened for years (I believe India's digitalization started in the 1990s Under the leadership of Rajeev Gandhi, PV Narasimha Rao, and Dr. Manmohan Singh), I fully agree and acknowledge the digital growth achieved in the last nine years under the leadership of Prime Minister Shri Modi.

The unprecedented growth in technology has reshaped the landscape of India, opening numerous opportunities and avenues for development. This book delves into the myriad facets of Digital India, exploring growth in each sector, from governance to entrepreneurship, E-commerce to Digital payment. As we navigate through this digital revolution, it is crucial to understand the challenges and ways to sustain this exponential growth.

Acknowledgements

I want to thank my family, especially my wife Vanishree, who always inspires me and my children, Manasa, Sanavi, and Sanat.

Sir Nandan Nilekani's presentation on India's Digital Transformation motivated me to write this book.

I also acknowledge the support from many AI tools like Grammarly, Open AI, Canvas, Google, etc., and many Indian government websites, which were immensely helpful.

About the Author

Dr. Rajeev Joshi is a professional in the field of Automation and Control. He has over 24 years of experience in engineering, plant maintenance, project, and program management. The author is a visiting professor at management institutes in Bangalore.

The author has an engineering degree and a Doctor of Business Administration in Strategic Management and Digital Transformation.

1. The Digital Revolution: Global Perspective

The digital revolution stands as one of the most transformative phenomena of the modern era, reshaping industries, economies, and societies on a global scale. The first chapter details the evolution of the digital revolution from a global perspective, tracing its roots, examining its key drivers, and exploring its far-reaching impacts. After understanding the international perspective, the author further focuses on India's unique position within this global narrative, highlighting its emergence as a prominent player in the digital landscape.

The seeds of the digital revolution were sown decades ago, with the advent of computing technology in the mid-20th century. The development of early computers laid the groundwork for the digitization of information and the automation of processes, setting the stage for the profound transformations that would follow. Around the 1950s and 60s, military establishments and scientific organizations of many countries started using computers to handle complex data and functions *1. However, it was still out of reach for the common man.

The beginning of the 1980s saw the digital concept gaining momentum with the introduction of automatic teller machines

(ATMs), industrial robots, video games, and computer-based images. As a result, people started buying computers for home use. In the same decade, in 1983, Motorola developed the first mobile phone, and the first digital camera was developed in 1988.

The subsequent proliferation of the internet in the late 20th century served as a catalyst for the digital revolution, facilitating the unprecedented exchange of information and connectivity across the globe. Tim Berners-Lee's invention of the World Wide Web (www) in 1989 marked a pivotal moment in this journey, democratizing access to information and laying the groundwork for the digital infrastructure that underpins our interconnected world today.

Key Drivers of the Digital Revolution:

Several key factors have driven the digital revolution forward, shaping its trajectory and accelerating its pace. Technological innovation lies at the heart of this transformation, with breakthroughs in computing power, connectivity, and software development fueling the continual evolution of digital technologies.

The rise of mobile computing, epitomized by the ubiquitous smartphone, has been particularly instrumental in extending the reach of the digital revolution to all corners of the globe. The proliferation of mobile devices has empowered individuals with unprecedented access to information, services, and opportunities, bridging geographic divides and transcending traditional barriers to communication and commerce. As per the Statista survey, by the end of 2023, there were more than 4.24 billion smartphone users worldwide, and it is expected to reach 6.24 billion by the year 2029*2.

Moreover, the emergence of cloud computing has revolutionized the way we store, process, and access data, enabling scalable and cost-effective solutions for businesses and individuals alike. The cloud has catalyzed the growth of new digital services and business models, empowering organizations to innovate and adapt in an increasingly dynamic and interconnected world.

As technology becomes more user-orientated and user-friendly, the public is becoming more digitally literate and starting to use technology and apply it in a number of areas of their lives. The digital revolution is reshaping social media, online shopping, web applications, remote working, and on-demand entertainment services.

Impacts of the Digital Revolution:

The digital revolution has exerted profound impacts across virtually every aspect of human endeavor, fundamentally reshaping the way we work, communicate, and live. In the realm of business and commerce, digital technologies have disrupted traditional industries and business models, giving rise to new forms of entrepreneurship, innovation, and economic value creation.

The democratization of information facilitated by the internet has empowered individuals with unprecedented access to knowledge and resources, fostering a culture of lifelong learning and self-improvement. Social media platforms have facilitated new modes of communication and collaboration, enabling the rapid dissemination of information and the formation of virtual communities transcending geographical boundaries.

Furthermore, the digital revolution has catalyzed significant shifts in governance and politics, empowering citizens with new tools for civic engagement and political participation. From grassroots social movements to online activism, digital technologies have played a pivotal role in amplifying voices and catalyzing social change on a global scale.

Resources:

1. https://courses.minnalearn.com/en/courses/digital-revolution/the-digital-revolution/what-is-the-digital-revolution/

2. https://www.statista.com/forecasts/1143723/smartphone-users-in-the-world

2. India's Position in Digital Landscape

India's digital transformation has been propelled by a confluence of factors, including government initiatives to promote digital inclusion and entrepreneurship, as well as the rapid adoption of mobile technology and internet services across the country. The proliferation of affordable smartphones and low-cost mobile data plans has democratized access to digital services, enabling millions of Indians to leapfrog traditional barriers to connectivity and participate in the digital economy.

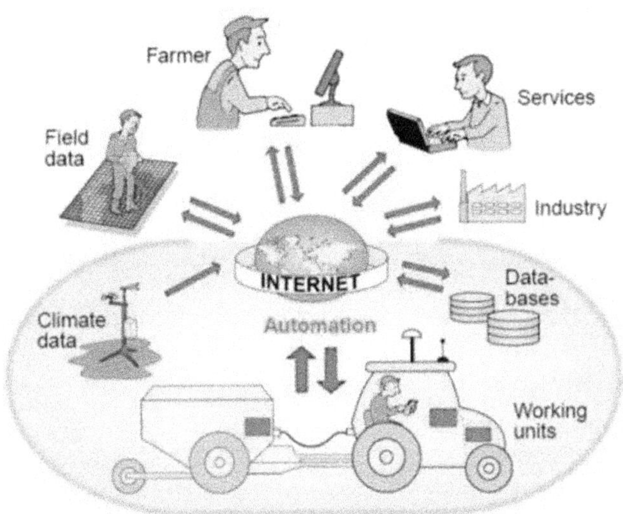

Source*1

Moreover, India's vibrant startup ecosystem has emerged as a hotbed of innovation and creativity, attracting investment and talent from around the world. From fintech and e-commerce to healthcare and education, Indian startups are leveraging digital technologies to address pressing societal challenges and unlock new opportunities for growth and prosperity.

Early Beginnings:

India's tryst with digital technology dates back to the late 20th century, when the government-initiated efforts to introduce computing infrastructure and expertise in the country. In the 1960s, India established the Indian Institutes of Technology (IITs), which played a crucial role in fostering indigenous research and development in the field of computer science and technology. These institutions laid the groundwork for India's emergence as a global hub for IT talent in the decades to come. The 1980s witnessed the launch of key initiatives such as the National Informatics Centre (NIC) and the Centre for Development of Advanced Computing (C-DAC), which aimed at promoting the adoption of computing technology in government institutions and foster indigenous research and development in critical areas such as supercomputing and software development.

Liberalization and Globalization:

The early 1990s marked a significant turning point in India's economic and technological trajectory. The introduction of economic liberalization policies opened up the country's markets to foreign investment and trade. The liberalization era paved the way for the entry of multinational corporations into India's burgeoning IT sector, catalyzing the growth of the software services industry and positioning India as a global outsourcing destination for IT and business process services.

The establishment of software technology parks and special economic zones further fuelled the growth of India's IT industry, providing companies with tax incentives and infrastructure support to set up operations in the country. This period saw the emergence of iconic Indian IT companies such as Infosys, TCS, and Wipro, which played a pivotal role in shaping India's digital landscape and establishing its reputation as a global technology powerhouse. Today the top 10 Indian IT companies together have market cap of Rs 28 Lakh crores and provide employment to 2.7 million professionals*2.

Digital Inclusion and Democratization:

Despite the remarkable progress made in the IT sector, India grappled with significant disparities in access to digital technologies across different segments of society. Recognizing the importance of bridging the digital divide, the government launched ambitious initiatives such as the National e-Governance Plan (NeGP) and the Digital India program, aimed at promoting digital inclusion and leveraging technology to deliver essential services to citizens across the country.

The proliferation of mobile technology and the advent of

affordable smartphones further accelerated the pace of digital inclusion in India, enabling millions of Indians to access the internet and digital services for the first time. The widespread adoption of mobile wallets and digital payment platforms revolutionized how Indians transact, driving financial inclusion and reducing reliance on cash-based transactions.

Startup Ecosystem and Innovation:

India's digital landscape is characterized by a vibrant and dynamic startup ecosystem fuelled by a potent mix of entrepreneurial talent, technological innovation, and supportive government policies. From e-commerce and fintech to health tech and edtech, Indian startups are leveraging digital technologies to address a diverse range of challenges and opportunities, driving innovation and disruption across various sectors of the economy.

Government initiatives such as Startup India and Atal Innovation Mission have played a crucial role in nurturing the startup ecosystem, providing funding, mentorship, and regulatory support to aspiring entrepreneurs and innovators. The emergence of startup hubs in cities like Bangalore, Hyderabad, and Mumbai has further catalyzed the growth of India's digital economy, attracting investment and talent from around the world.

Challenges and Opportunities:

While India has made significant strides in the digital landscape, it continues to face various challenges that threaten to impede its progress. Issues such as digital literacy, cybersecurity, and privacy concerns pose significant hurdles to the widespread adoption of digital technologies across the country. Moreover, the digital divide persists, with rural and marginalized communities still needing access to basic digital infrastructure and services.

However, amidst these challenges lie tremendous opportunities for India to leverage its unique position in the digital landscape to drive inclusive growth and development. By harnessing the power of emerging technologies such as artificial intelligence, blockchain, and the Internet of Things, India can unlock new avenues for innovation and transformation across sectors such as healthcare, agriculture, and education. Chapters 10 and 11 discuss in detail the challenges and strategies to sustain Indian digital growth.

Resources:

1. https://www.insightsonindia.com/2019/01/08/insights-into-editorial-its-time-to-reimagine-social-impact-in-a-digital-india/

2. https://www.forbesindia.com/article/explainers/top-10-it-companies-in-india/87143/1

3. Key Digital Technologies

The technology encompassed in DT solutions covers a broad range, including cloud computing, data analysis, IoT, and AI. Organizations repeatedly had to utilize these technologies to remain up to date.

Aside from improving processes, digital technology may offer new means of communicating with clients and making choices. Just the same, it contributes much in ways unchronicled elsewhere to an understanding of market trends. This seismic change not only forces businesses to go back to square one, modify tactics, and embrace the digital world, but it also has them scrambling with each other for innovation. This launch signifies the start of a new era where enterprises must strategically adopt digital technology to thrive and succeed.

 Let us have a look at some promising digital technologies.

RPA:

Robotic process automation (RPA) is a vital technological central to realizing a successful digital transformation. RPA is a toolbox-based technology that employs software robots or bots to enhance manual, repetitive, or rule-bound business operations by interacting with computers in the same way humans do. Many businesses doing everything from assembly work to surgery will be radically altered in terms of precision, scalability, and other operating characteristics.

RPA's forte consists of helping to raise productivity, reduce operating costs, and increase operational efficiency. Automation of low-level and repetitive activities can free people from tasks to devote their energies to higher-level, more strategic activities. Under these circumstances, RPA can be blended seamlessly with existing systems and applications; it provides a convenient way for companies to update without having to give their whole system a gut job.

Moreover, RPA can help lower the possibility of human error and increase accuracy and compliance. Besides that, it just makes everything easier to do. You can make all kinds of decisions faster and more conveniently and adapt to the market. While companies embark upon digital transformation, RPA can also be deliberately employed to engender operational excellence and spur creativity. This would likewise be a reasonable basis for receiving future technology. Its unparalleled versatility and productivity make RPA a central pillar of any genuinely effective digital transformation efforts.

IIOT:

The industrial Internet of Things (IIoT) is the new crest in this whole wave and refers to digital transformation for industry. The IIoT is all about bringing smart devices, sensors and linked systems into industry so that large amounts of information can be gathered in real time, analysed and used. The network-based ecosystem structure promotes operational performance and innovation through increasing transparency, simplifying operations, and making better decisions. The digital transformation of manufacturing and industrial processes is closely related to the development of IIoT. In addition to these methods, it also enables companies to improve overall manufacturing effectiveness and enter a new paradise of production. By monitoring sensors on machinery, the IIoT system can assist with predictive maintenance. Fault prediction can reduce downtime and increase overall equipment performance.

Further, because the information generated by IIoT can assist businesses in using big data analytics to increase operating efficiency and reduce costs (such as electricity) or improve supply chain management. Moreover, by integrating into industrial operations, the IIoT not only makes procedures simpler but also smooths the way for smart factories, which help industries automate and network together to change completely modern-day production. In effect, the IIoT is, in fact, a motor for industrial digital transformation--allowing companies to use data-driven approaches and be more agile at competitive times when competition abounds.

MES:

Manufacturing Execution System (MES) is vital for digital transformation in the manufacturing industry. MES bridges the gap between enterprise-level planning systems and the shop floor. It is a complete software solution that orchestrates and monitors manufacturing activities in real-time. This technology dramatically improves productivity, excellence, and promptness in production.

MES data, which comes from sensors, machines, and human input, provides a holistic view of the production process. The monitoring and control capabilities of MES make increased productivity and the elimination of process bottlenecks possible. As an extra benefit, this can provide data-driven recommendations. This allows for more variable manufacturing, allowing companies to adjust swiftly to market and consumer demand changes.

Integration, automation, and data-driven intelligence are the key principles that drive digital transformation. It can incorporate various emerging technologies, like the Internet of

Things (IoT) and artificial intelligence, to further enhance its capabilities. In the middle of the chaos of contemporary manufacturing processes, managers who use MES may achieve more streamlined digital workflows, improved customer response, and more traceability.

ERP:

ERP is a inclusive software package that promotes organic stations in management and streamlining their processes. But technologies that unify information such as enterprise resource planning (ERP), which combines data management activities to keep various systems in step, play an extremely significant role. An ERP system is a central access point that links important company functions, such as accounting, human resources (HR), manufacturing operations, and supply chain management. These may also include the customer relationship management function of CRM (customer relations-management). ERP systems remove departmental silos by centralizing data and procedures, which maximizes productivity.

Today, an ERP system is a must as companies gear up for the digital age. Today's modern enterprise resource planning solutions scale value as a business. Cloud computing, AI, and data analytics help achieve this effect. In addition, new cloud

ERPs provide real-time feedback so companies know precisely how to serve clients best. It will help digital businesses compete and adjust quickly according to changing market conditions while making data-based decisions.

ERP is a strategic enabler, and successful digital transformer smoothly integrate it into their overall strategy. This integration assists the organization in process standardization, optimizing operations, and responding to a digital business landscape. It also underpins interoperability and data consistency.

Digital Twins:

The idea of digital twins, with its ability to create a digital stand-in for real objects, processes, or systems within all operations, is truly revolutionary for effectively using data. A digital twin is an electronic version of a physical object that can replicate its actions and characteristics in real time. This technology is critical to better decision-making, predictive maintenance, and operational efficiency in many industries. Under the conditions of digital transformation, Digital Twins offer unprecedented insight into the state and productivity of assets and procedures. They allow companies to analyse, monitor, and improve processes more accurately and quickly than before. For example, a Digital Twin of a manufacturing line can simulate various conditions to improve efficiency and reduce downtime by optimizing the workflow or predicting when maintenance is needed.

Furthermore, Digital Twins leverages IoT sensors and real-time data inputs to enhance the scope of data-driven projects. Therefore, businesses can better anticipate customer needs, improve product development, and react promptly to changing market conditions. In the age of Industry 4.0, Digital Twins are genuinely a game-changer for organizations. They use these tools to achieve a digital yet successful and flexible future.

Cybersecurity:

If digital transformation is going to succeed, everyone has to take action on cybersecurity because the attacker changes strategy constantly. All the methods, means, and procedures for protecting computer systems, networks, and data from hackers and other assailants are grouped under cybersecurity. As more and more organizations embark on digital transformation, introduce cloud applications, or use technologies like the Internet of Things (IoT) or artificial intelligence (AI), the size of their attack surface is getting bigger. Establishing Trust in Digital Ecosystems Through effective cybersecurity, we must secure sensitive information's availability, integrity, and confidentiality. To do this, precautions like encryption, access limitations, and regular security audits are required. A solid digital infrastructure creates a safe environment for the implementation of new technologies, enabling organisations to capitalise on the benefits of digitalization securely. The fact is that cybersecurity is about more than simply protection.

Companies must prioritize challenges related to fast emerging cyber dangers from the very beginning of their digital strategy planning. Setting up asset protection as a strategy to increase resilience, thereby enacting an active and holistic cybersecurity approach, is the way for organizations of all types wanting to traipse through this forest of digital disorder with less fear. Thus, they can carry on their metamorphosis work well.

Cloud:

Cloud computing refers to storing, processing, and using applications via the Internet. It offers excellent scalability, flexibility, and accessibility--three essentials for game-changing programs. Digital transformation is changing the name of pace and profit-taking. The cloud changes it all again? This allows businesses to bypass the limitations imposed on them, enabling the shortening of deployment timescales for applications and services. Pay-as-you-go pricing in cloud computing strengthens financial predictability by turning capital expenses into operating costs and optimizing cost structures.

When connected to the Internet, a cloud can reach into various corners of cyberspace and access people's data or applications around abolishing new businesses. It is also the processing power required to keep up with vast amounts of information and, therefore, an important product for technologies that rely on large volumes of data, such as big data analysis, AI, or machine learning. Cloud solutions can also enhance security in many other ways. For instance, they make it possible for data to be routinely encrypted and regularly updated with the latest protocols following management guidelines instituted by centralized authorities. In addition to complying with the regulations, it also takes steps toward guarding sensitive information. Lying at the heart of this game-changing possibility is innovation and other capabilities that firms possess. No other establishment can achieve DT success like the cloud.

AI, ML, and DL:

AI, ML, and DL are the key components of digital transformation. The field of study and engineering absorbed in creating intelligent systems is known as Artificial intelligence; these programs are used for computers that can reflect the thinking behavior of humans.

Machine learning is the branch of AI that empowers computers to boost their efficiency without human involvement. Deep Learning (DL) is subset of ML.

To analyse and digest complicated data, deep learning is a division of ML that uses the same type of neural network as traditional machine intelligence—employee responsibility 1. Helps decision-making and reduces the work of complex procedures; 2. It enhances human potential, encouraging people to be more creative in their productivity at work. Differentiation of large-scale data uses computer learning methods to further clarify decision-making based on facts. DL's ability to analyse quantities accurately and its pattern analysis and correlation capabilities fit it very well for two other areas: image recognition, which requires shape identification, and voice entry. This is where DL improves the user experience.

AI, ML, and DL facilitate companies' adaptation to the online world. Procedure optimization, personalized customer experiences, and innovation encouragement give them a competitive edge in today's ever-changing markets. By adequately harnessing these digital technologies, businesses can fully use data and turn it into an asset for long-term growth.

Drones:

Drones, officially called Unmanned Aerial Vehicles (UAVs), are aircraft or flying devices with no human pilots. These devices are controlled remotely by human pilots or computers. Initially, drones were used only by the military, but now they are used in business, delivery, horticultural, and agricultural applications. As technology evolves, drones will become safer and more dependable.

4. **Pre-Digital Era in India**

A complex interplay of historical, social, and economic factors has shaped India's journey into the digital age. To truly understand India's digital growth story, it's essential to examine the technological landscape that existed before the advent of digital technologies. This chapter explores India's pre-digital era, tracing the country's technology evolution and highlighting the factors that laid the groundwork for its digital transformation.

Technological Landscape Before the Digital Era:

India has a rich history of technological innovation that predates the digital revolution. From ancient achievements in mathematics and astronomy to advancements in metallurgy and textiles, Indian civilization has long been at the forefront of scientific and technological progress. However, the modern era of technology in India began to take shape during the colonial period, with the introduction of Western scientific ideas and industrial technologies.

The British Raj brought with it significant infrastructure developments such as railways, telegraphs, and postal services, which played a crucial role in facilitating communication and commerce across the vast expanse of the Indian subcontinent. These technological advancements laid the foundation for

India's integration into the global economy and provided the impetus for further innovation and modernization in the years to come.

Industrialization and Technological Modernization:

The post-independence period saw India embark on a path of industrialization and technological modernization aimed at achieving self-sufficiency and economic development. The establishment of institutions such as the Indian Institutes of Technology (IITs) and the Council of Scientific and Industrial Research (CSIR) signaled the government's commitment to promoting indigenous research and innovation in science and technology.

Key sectors such as agriculture, manufacturing, and infrastructure witnessed significant technological advancements during this period, driven by initiatives such as the Green Revolution and the development of public sector enterprises in strategic industries. However, India's technological progress remained constrained by factors such as limited access to capital, bureaucratic red tape, and a need for coordination between academia, industry, and government.

The Role of Public Sector Enterprises:

One of the defining features of India's pre-digital technological landscape was the prominent role played by public sector enterprises (PSEs) in driving innovation and industrial growth.

Government-owned entities such as Bharat Heavy Electricals Limited (BHEL), Hindustan Aeronautics Limited (HAL), and Indian Space Research Organisation (ISRO) spearheaded groundbreaking projects in sectors ranging from power generation to aerospace.

ISRO, in particular, emerged as a symbol of India's technological prowess with its successful satellite launches and the development of indigenous space exploration capabilities. The organization's achievements showcased India's scientific and engineering talent and demonstrated the potential for collaboration between the public and private sectors in advancing technological innovation.

When other countries, especially the USA, did not provide technological support, India tried to develop using indigenous resources. For instance, the journey to a supercomputer began when India was denied access to the CRAY supercomputer in the mid-eighties. In 1998, C-DAC launched PARAM 10,000, demonstrating India's capacity to build 100 gigaflop machines*1.

Indian economy started changing after the 1991 liberalization moves from then finance minister Dr. Manmohan Singh under the leadership of Prime Minister PV Narasimha Rao. Just before that Liberalization moved in Aug 1991, India was forced to pledge 67 tonnes of gold to secure the loan. In the Budget speech, Manmohan Singh ji said, "I do not minimize the difficulties that lie ahead on the long and arduous journey on which we have embarked. But as Victor Hugo once said, "No power on earth can stop an idea whose time has come. I suggest to this august House that the emergence of India as a major economic power in the world happens to be one such idea. Let the whole world hear it loud and clear. India is now wide awake. We shall prevail. We shall overcome". What happened next is the historical decision taken on that day, and it forever changed the lives of Indians as the country embarked upon a new journey*2.

As a result of liberalization, foreign company direct investment (FDI) started increasing, and development in technology started due to foreign technology in industrial applications. Today, almost all IT MNCs have branches and R&D offices in India. Indian IT professionals are the most driving force in the world's digital revolution. The world's most valued IT companies, like Google and Microsoft, are led by CEOs of Indian origin. Indian IT giants like TCS, Infosys, Wipro, and HCL are the most recognized companies in the world.

Challenges and Limitations:
Despite the strides made in various sectors, India's pre-digital technological landscape was characterized by several challenges and limitations that hindered its full potential. A

lack of investment in research and development, inadequate infrastructure, and a shortage of skilled manpower were among the key barriers to technological advancement in the country.

Moreover, India's reliance on imported technologies and equipment underscored the need for greater emphasis on indigenous innovation and self-reliance. The inefficiencies of the public sector, coupled with bureaucratic inertia and regulatory constraints, further impeded the pace of technological progress and stifled entrepreneurial initiatives.

Resources:
1. https://mashelkar.com/articles/indias-technology-journey/
2. https://economictimes.indiatimes.com/news/economy/policy/on-this-day-in-1991-a-landmark-budget-that-changed-indias-fortunes/articleshow/93090439.cms?utm_source=contentofinterest&utm_medium=text&utm_campaign=cppst

5. Government Policies and Initiatives

Current and previous governments have played pivotal roles by launching new initiatives and policies. India's journey in the digital domain began with a series of pioneering initiatives aimed at leveraging technology for economic development, social empowerment, and administrative efficiency. Early digital initiatives undertaken in India and the policy framework laid the foundation for its subsequent digital growth story.

National Informatics Centre (NIC):

Established in 1976, the NIC played an important role in providing technological support to government departments and agencies. NIC developed critical infrastructure such as computer networks, databases, and software applications to facilitate information sharing and decision-making within the government. NIC contributes to rapid advancements in ICT technologies such as Mobility, Cloud, Big Data, Artificial Intelligence, Blockchain, and the Internet of Things (IoT)*4.

Indian Institutes of Technology (IITs):

Founded in the 1950s and 1960s, the IITs emerged as premier institutions for technical education and research. IIT's Produces a pool of talented engineers and scientists who are contributing to India's burgeoning IT industry.

Centre for Development of Advanced Computing (C-DAC):

C-DAC was Established in 1988 with the main aim of developing the super computers, since USA denied it for India. Today C-DAC focuses on research and development in high-performance computing, networking, and software technology. It played a crucial role in developing indigenous computing solutions and building India's expertise in critical areas of information technology[5].

Education and Training Programs:

Various government-sponsored programs and initiatives were launched to promote computer literacy and IT skills among the Indian population. The introduction of computer education in schools and colleges has helped to create a skilled workforce capable of driving India's digital transformation.

Information Technology Act, 2000:

The information technology act was introduced in 2000 to provide legal recognition for electronic transactions and facilitate e-governance initiatives. Act established regulatory frameworks for digital signatures, cybercrime, and data protection, it laid the groundwork for a secure and conducive environment for digital transactions[7].

National Telecom Policy, 1999:

The National Telcom Policy, introduced in 1999, aims to

liberalize and deregulate India's telecom sector to promote competition, innovation, and investment. The objective is to provide affordable and effective means of telecommunication for all citizens. This policy led to significant telecom infrastructure expansion and modernization, paving the way for increased connectivity and internet penetration across the country*8.

National e-Governance Plan (NeGP):

Launched in 2006, NeGP aimed to transform the delivery of government services using information technology. To promote e-Governance in a holistic manner, various policy initiatives and projects have been undertaken to develop core and support infrastructure. The major core infrastructure components are State Data Centres (SDCs), State Wide Area Networks (S.W.A.N), Common Services Centres (CSCs) and middleware gateways i.e National e-Governance Service Delivery Gateway (NSDG), State e-Governance Service Delivery Gateway (SSDG), and Mobile e-Governance Service Delivery Gateway (MSDG)*9.

CRIME AND CRIMINAL TRACKING NETWORK & SYSTEMS (CCTNS):

CCTNS has the vision of creating a comprehensive and integrated system for enhancing the efficiency and effectiveness of policing through adopting the principle of e-governance and the creation of a nationwide networking infrastructure for the evolution of a state-of-the-art tracking system around the 'Investigation of crime and detection of criminals' *13.

Digital India Initiative:

Digital India is a flagship project that Prime Minister Mr. Modi launched in 2015. It started with the vision of transforming India into a digitally empowered society and knowledge economy. It is focused on three key areas: 1. Digital infrastructure as a utility for every Indian 2. Governance and services on demand 3. Digital empowerment of citizens. There are nine pillars in Digital India, which the government is hoping to achieve within a fixed timeline. Each pillar has a specific cause and budget to implement *6.

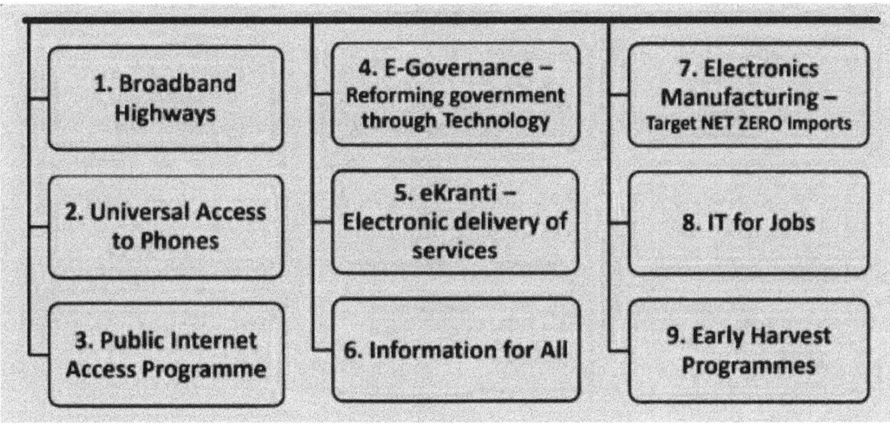

Fig: Nine Pillars Digital India

Aadhaar:

Introduced in 2009, Aadhaar is a biometric identification system that provides a unique identity to Indian residents based on their demographic and biometric information. Infosys co-founder Mr. Nandan Nilekani was responsible for this government flagship program. As explained by Nilekani in one of the conferences when he took over as the in charge of Aadhar, just a piece of paper was given to him with the mandate of a unique ID for citizens' Aadhaar. It was Nilekani visionary who introduced digital ID or digital Aadhar. Aadhar has facilitated targeted service delivery, improved efficiency, and reduced leakages in government welfare programs, contributing to financial inclusion and social empowerment. Aadhar (which means pillar) is now the base for many applications in India. Today, India runs the world's largest direct benefit program, which is helping 700 million people. Government initiative Jan Dhan Yojana has reduced corruption, and the amount directly reaches the beneficiaries. At present 100000+ crores have been transferred effortlessly, automatically, and in real-time. It was also used in COWIN platform for Covid-19 vaccination. The platform allowed Indian citizens to book vaccinations and get digital vaccination certificates. Today, 1.3 Billion Indian has Aadhar identity; it is used not only for government programs but also as the primary document in e-KYC (Know your customer). As per the estimation, around 80 million transactions are done daily using Aadhar *3.

Role of Demonetization and Covid-19:

Demonization and Covid-19 played pivotal roles in India's digitization and digital economy. Demonetization drive by the government in 2016 involved the withdrawal of high-denomination banknotes; this led to a cash crunch and forced citizens to adopt digital payment methods. As per RBI, digital transactions increased from 2,80,000 in November 2016 to 40,10,000 in November 2020. The Covid-19 pandemic due to social distancing requirements further forced people to adopt digital payment*15.

In fact, COVID-19 did not impact India's digitization drive but affected the entire world. All business leaders started thinking about digital transformation of their business processes. In the words of Steve Hasker, president and CEO of Thomas Reuters Corp, "I think we have seen three to four years of progress in just three to four months, in terms of acceptance of what the new world needs to look like" *16.

Make in India:

Launched in 2014, Make in India aims to promote domestic manufacturing and position India as a global manufacturing hub. Which includes initiatives such as the Electronics

Manufacturing Cluster (EMC) scheme, that provides infrastructure and incentives to attract investment in electronics manufacturing.

Recently, India has also actively attracted both domestic and international companies to invest in semiconductor manufacturing. Indian Prime Minister Mr. Modi's vision is to make India a semiconductor hub. Tata Electronics Private Limited ("TEPL") has decided to invest Rs 91K crores to set up a semiconductor fab in partnership with Powerchip Semiconductor Manufacturing Corp (PSMC), Taiwan, in Dholera, Gujarat*1.

Startup India:

Launched in 2016, Startup India aims to foster entrepreneurship and promote innovation by providing funding, mentorship, and regulatory support to startups. This includes initiatives such as the Startup India Seed Fund Scheme and the Atal Innovation Mission, which provide financial and logistical support to startups and innovators. The Startup India Seed Fund Scheme (SISFS) has been approved with a corpus of Rs. 945 crore for the period of 4 years starting from 2021-22. At the end of 2022, SISFS distributed more than Rs 480 crores for eligible 133 incubators*2.

ACCESSIBLE INDIA CAMPAIGN AND MOBILE APP:

Sugamya Bharat Abhiyaan, or Accessible India Campaign, is an initiative of the Department of Empowerment of Persons with Disabilities (DEPwD), Ministry of Social Justice & Empowerment. It aims to enable people with disabilities to access equal opportunity, live independently, and participate fully in all aspects of life in an inclusive society. The mobile application is a crowd-sourcing platform that comprehensively obtains information on inaccessible places across the country. The mobile application is available on IOS, Android, and Windows platforms and can be downloaded from the respective App Stores*10.

BHIM (BHARAT INTERFACE FOR MONEY):

Bharat Interface for Money (BHIM) is an app that makes payment transactions simple, easy, and quick using Unified Payments Interface (UPI). It enables direct bank-to-bank payments instantly and collects money using a Mobile number or Payment address. Bhim is used for instant bank-to-bank payments and to pay and collect money using just a mobile number or virtual payment address (UPI ID). As of Feb 2024, the number of banks live on this app was 412, with a volume of 22.5 million*11.

AGRIMARKET APP:

This mobile App was developed to keep farmers abreast of crop prices and discourage them from carrying out distress sales. Through this App, Farmers can get information related to crop prices in markets within 50km of their own device. This App is currently available in Hindi and English, and prices of agri commodities are sourced from the Agmarknet portal*12.

DIGITAL AIIMS:

The Digital AIIMS project was initiated in January 2015 with the aim of effective linkage between AIIMS, the Unique Identification Authority of India (UIDAI), and the Ministry of Electronics and Information Technology (MeiTY). A Unique health identification (ID) for every patient visiting AIIMS will be generated on the Aadhar platform. This ID is given to every patient visiting AIIMS to maintain his/her digital identity*14.

Regulatory Challenges and Responses:

Government policies and initiatives have played a crucial role in fostering digital growth and driving socio-economic development in India. By providing the necessary regulatory frameworks, infrastructure, and support mechanisms, the Indian government has created an enabling environment for the adoption and diffusion of digital technologies across various sectors of the economy. As India continues on its digital journey, it must build upon these initiatives by fostering innovation, promoting inclusivity, and addressing emerging challenges to realize its vision of a truly digital and empowered nation.

Resources:

1. https://www.zeebiz.com/companies/news-tata-group-to-start-semiconductor-chips-production-from-gujarat

2. https://pib.gov.in/PressReleasePage.aspx?PRID=1895966

3. Nandan Nilekani On Digital India: "From Offline To Online, Formal,MegaEconomy".
https://www.youtube.com/watch?v=LTlJl0xWg_M.

4. https://www.nic.in/

5. https://www.cdac.in/index.aspx?id=about

6. https://digitalindiainsight.com/9-pillars-of-digital-india/

7. https://www.indiacode.nic.in/

8.https://cis-india.org/telecom/resources/new-telecom-policy-1999

9.https://www.meity.gov.in/divisions/national-e-governance-plan

10 https://sugamyabharat.gov.in/

11.https://www.npci.org.in/what-we-do/bhim/product-statistics

12. http://mkisan.gov.in/downloadmobileapps.aspx

13.
http://www.ncrb.gov.in/BureauDivisions/CCTNS/cctns.htm

14. http://ehospital.nic.in/ehospital/

15.https://www.linkedin.com/pulse/rise-digital-payments-india-after-demonetisation-vitwo/

16.
https://kpmg.com/us/en/home/insights/2020/09/digital-acceleration.html

6. Infrastructure Development: Catalyst for Growth

Infrastructure development has been a cornerstone of India's digital growth story, laying the foundation for connectivity, accessibility, and innovation in the digital domain.

Telecommunications Infrastructure:

The liberalization of India's telecom sector in the 1990s paved the way for significant investments in telecommunications infrastructure.

The establishment of the Telecom Regulatory Authority of India (TRAI) helped regulate the sector and promote competition, expanding mobile and broadband networks across the country.

Initiatives such as the National Telecom Policy and BharatNet have aimed to bridge the digital divide by providing affordable and accessible connectivity to rural and underserved areas. One mission of BharatNet was to provide broadband connectivity to over 250,000 gram panchayats covering 625,000 villages through the National Optical Fibre Network (NOFN) across India.

As of the end of the year 2023, the government has connected approximately 194,000 villages, providing internet access to around 5,67,000 households. Through new BharatNet Udyami project 3,51,000 fibre connections have been established.

The below table shows the status of BharatNet usage by the end of March 2024*1:

Activities	Volume
Wifi hot spot GPs installed	1, 04,675
FTTH commissioned	9, 66, 213
Dark Fibre installed (km)	82, 311.45
Wifi/FTTH data consumption (TB)	1, 05, 959

The telecom industry in India is the second largest in the world, with a subscriber base of 1.084 Billion as of February 2024 (wireless + wireline subscribers). According to the survey, India has an overall tele density of 85.23%. The urban market's tele density seems to be saturated at 133.76%, whereas the rural market is still untapped at 58.56% *2.

Internet Backbone and Connectivity:

India's internet backbone infrastructure has undergone significant expansion and modernization over the years, driven by public and private investments.

Undersea cable projects such as SEA-ME-WE and EIG have enhanced international connectivity, facilitating high-speed internet access and data exchange with the global community.

Initiatives like the National Optical Fibre Network (NOFN) and BharatNet aim to extend broadband connectivity to remote and rural areas, enabling last-mile access to digital services and information.

As per Nokia's annual Mobile Broadband Index (MBiT) report, India's investment in private wireless networks is expected to reach around $250 million by 2027*3. Another report from Google, Temasek, and Bain & Company shows that India's internet economy is expected to grow sixfold to $1 trillion by 2030 from $175 to $1 trillion by 2030 from $175 billion in 2022. In the same duration, the internet economy contribution to Indian GDP is expected to increase from the current 4-5% to 12-13%*5.

According to the Economic Times (ET) recent survey (2024), India now has 820 million active internet users, half of whom are from rural areas, a great shift compared to 2021. As shown in the graph below, there has been steady growth in rural India's internet usage from 2021 to 2023 * 4.

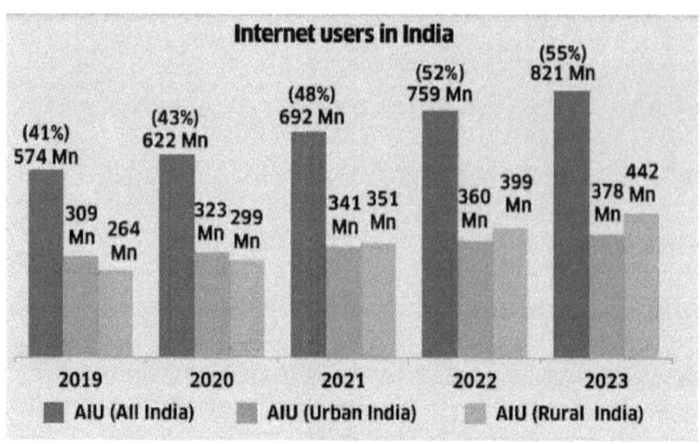

Source*4

Regarding mobile network providers 4G and 5G, Reliance Jio and Bharati Airtel are the market leaders. Together, Jio and Airtel have a market share of 72% of the Indian mobile market. Jio has a market share of 37%, and Airtel has around 35%. Vodaphone has 19%, and state-owned BSNL has 8%.

Digital Literacy and Skill Development:

In parallel with infrastructure development, efforts have been made to enhance digital literacy and skill development among the Indian population.

The Digital India initiative includes programs such as the Pradhan Mantri Gramin Digital Saksharta Abhiyan (PMGDISHA), which aims to provide digital literacy training to rural citizens.

Skill development initiatives in collaboration with industry partners and educational institutions aim to equip individuals with the necessary skills to participate in the digital economy.

In 2023, India launched another flagship project, "Skill India Digital (SID)". SID is a digital platform with a vision of synergizing and transforming India's skills, education, employment, and entrepreneurship landscape. Driven by the target to make skill development more innovative, SID focuses on digital technology and Industry 4.0 skills. The state-of the-art platform will be a breakthrough in accelerating skilled talent hiring, facilitating lifelong learning and career advancement*6. The below data from Statista shows the total number of trained beneficiaries under the digital literacy scheme. Over 63 million people have received training in digital literacy cumulatively since the financial year 2018*7.

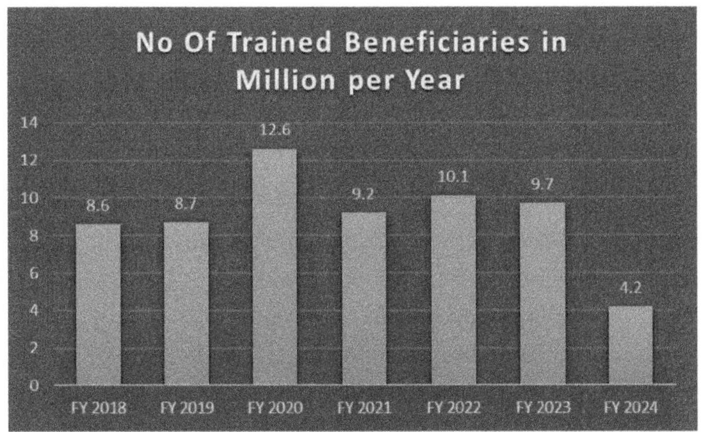

Source*7

According to a survey by the Ministry of Labor & Employment, Govt. of India, only 38% of households in India are digitally literate. In urban areas, digital literacy is relatively better, at 61%, as compared to 25% in rural areas.

Projects like SWAYAM offer Massive Online Open Courses (MOOCs) to leverage e-education. Swayam is an e-platform that facilitates hosting all courses taught in classrooms from Class 9 to post-graduation with open access. The scheme will provide 20 hours of basic training on digital devices and the internet and how to use these tools to avail government-enabled e-services, with a special focus on cashless transactions*8.

DigiLockers:

The mission of DigiLocker is paperless governance. Through digiLocker, the government wants to make document issuance and verification entirely online. Individuals can fetch their Aadhaar, driving license, educational certificates, PAN, etc., from the respective government departments, maintain them safely, and use them when required. Documents fetched are authentic as these are sourced directly from the official source. Online document storage provides convenience to people as they only need to carry the documents in some places. Currently as per the DigiLocker website 171.76 million DigiLocker users exists, and 5.62 billion documents are issued under different categories*11.

The below graphs show the year-wise use registration for DigiLocker and issued documents. During COVID-19, the growth was rapid, and later, it became steady.

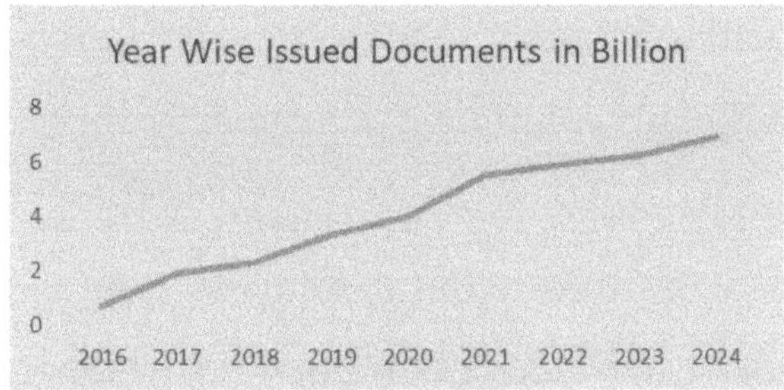

Source*12

Cloud Computing and Data Centers:

The proliferation of cloud computing has led to establishing data centers and cloud infrastructure across India. Global tech giants like Amazon Web Services (AWS), Microsoft Azure, and Google Cloud have invested in building data centers in India to cater to the growing demand for cloud services. The development of indigenous cloud platforms such as National Informatics Centre (NIC) Cloud and MeghRaj aims to promote data sovereignty and facilitate digital governance.

As per the "Research and Markets" analysis, India's data center market is set for robust growth, focusing on digital transformation and renewable energy integration. The market is expected to grow from the current 5.45 Billion $ to 7.02 Billion $ by 2027. The report observes that India stands as a global data hub, with an ecosystem conducive to the burgeoning demands of the digital age*9.

Smart Cities and IoT Infrastructure:

The Smart Cities Mission aims to transform urban areas into technologically advanced and sustainable innovation hubs. Smart city projects involve deploying IoT sensors, smart grids, and intelligent transportation systems to improve efficiency, enhance quality of life, and reduce environmental impact. Initiatives such as the Smart Cities Data Maturity Framework (SCDMF) aim to leverage data analytics and artificial intelligence to drive informed decision-making and optimize resource allocation in smart cities.

Despite government push and heavy investment, progress on smart cities has been slow. The table below provides a snapshot of the current status of Smart City Projects*10.

Progress Evaluation of SMART City Misison	
Total Projects and Investments	7,970 projects worth ₹1,70,400 crore
Completed Projects:	6,419 projects worth ₹1,25,105 crore
Projects at Work Order Stage	1,551 projects worth ₹45,295 crore.
Wifi/FTTH data consumption (TB)	1, 05, 959
100% Project Completed Cities	Madurai
More than 80% of work completion	56 cities
Cities Lagging Behind	Progress was 50% or below in 14 cities

Source *10.

Infrastructure development has been instrumental in catalyzing India's digital growth, enabling connectivity, accessibility, and innovation across the country. Continued investments in telecommunications, internet backbone, digital literacy, cloud computing, and smart city infrastructure are essential to sustain India's momentum towards digital transformation and realize its vision of a digitally empowered nation. Collaboration between government, industry, and other stakeholders will be key to overcoming challenges and unlocking the full potential of India's digital infrastructure in the years to come.

Resources:

1. https://bbnl.nic.in/usage2.pdf

2. https://www.investindia.gov.in/sector/telecom

3. https://www.livemint.com/news/india/indias-investment-in-pvt-wireless-network-to-be-at-250-mn-by-2027-report-11676546271668.html

4. https://economictimes.indiatimes.com/tech/technology/how-india-is-using-the-internet/articleshow/108354854.cms?utm_source=contentofinterest&utm_medium=text&utm_campaign=cppst

5. http://timesofindia.indiatimes.com/articleshow/1008
   08673.cms?utm_source=contentofinterest&utm_mediu
   m=text&utm_campaign=cppst

6. https://pib.gov.in/PressReleaseIframePage.aspx?PRID
   =1957139

7. https://www.statista.com/statistics/1196927/india-
   trained-beneficiaries-in-digital-literacy-scheme/

8. https://dtnbwed.cbwe.gov.in/images/upload/Digital
   -Literacy_3ZNK.pdf

9. https://www.researchandmarkets.com/reports/58919
   90/india-data-center-market-competition-forecast-

10. https://pwonlyias.com/current-affairs/smart-cities-
    mission-scm/

11. https://business.outlookindia.com/economy-and-
    policy/what-is-a-digilocker-how-to-open-it-and-what-
    are-the-benefits-

12. https://wb.digilocker.gov.in/statistics

7. The Rise of E-Commerce Platforms

The rise of e-commerce platforms in India represents a transformative shift in the country's retail and commerce landscape, ushering in new opportunities, challenges, and disruptions. E-commerce in India started with nascent beginnings and at current it is the booming industry driving digital growth and consumer empowerment.

Emergence of E-commerce:

K.Vaitheeswaran is the key person behind the growth of E-Commerce in India. He is popularly known as the 'Father of e-commerce in India' and cofounded Fabmart.com in 1999. After seeing the merits in the sector, other companies started showing interest.

The early 2000s witnessed the emergence of pioneering e-commerce platforms in India, such as Rediff Shopping and IndiaMart, catering primarily to niche markets and B2B transactions. However, the real turning point came with the launch of Flipkart in 2007, which revolutionized the Indian e-commerce landscape with its focus on customer experience, product selection, and logistics innovation.

Mobile Revolution and Growth of M-commerce:

The proliferation of smartphones and mobile internet access has fueled the growth of mobile commerce (m-commerce) in

India. E-commerce platforms have launched mobile apps and optimized their websites for mobile devices, catering to the growing number of consumers who prefer to shop on-the-go.

Flipkart's Dominance and Competition:

Flipkart's rapid growth and success paved the way for other e-commerce players to enter the market, including Amazon, Snapdeal, and Paytm Mall. Intense competition ensued, leading to aggressive pricing strategies, marketing campaigns, and investments in technology and infrastructure to capture market share. The chart below shows India's ten major market players and their revenue.

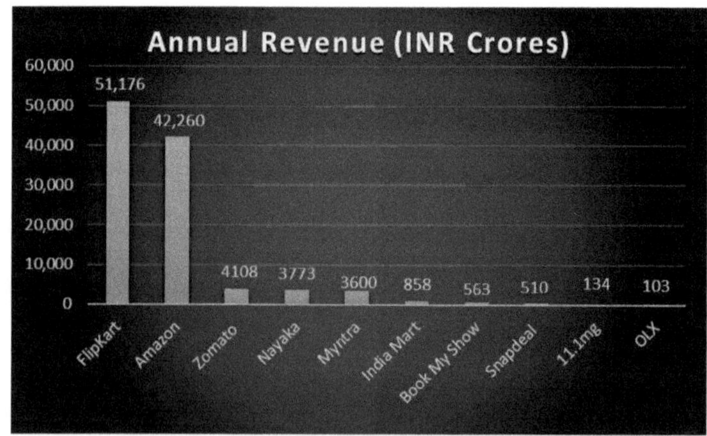

Source *1

According to the report Flipkart tops the online shopping market in India, with close to 50% market share.

The overall e-commerce market is also expected to reach US$350 billion by 2030. With over 800 million users, India was the second-largest internet market in the world, with 125.94

lakh crore UPI transactions in 2022.

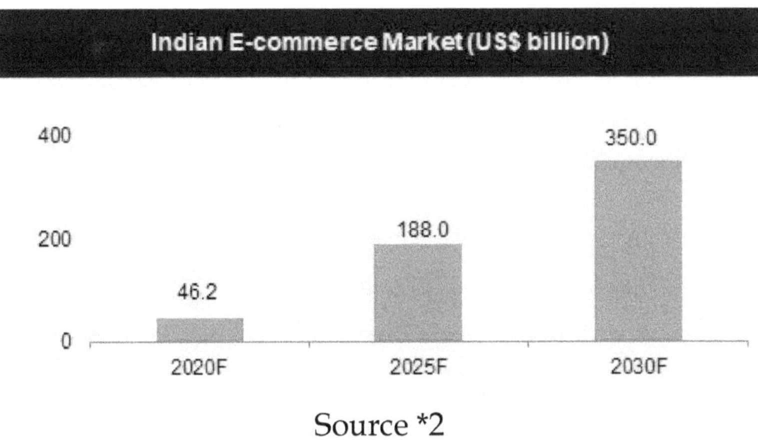

Source *2

Earlier, people preferred cash transactions, fearing security concerns with internet payments. However, Young India prefers online payments, and digital payments are predicted to account for a third of overall transactions in India by 2025. The graph below shows how Indians are spending online in each sector.

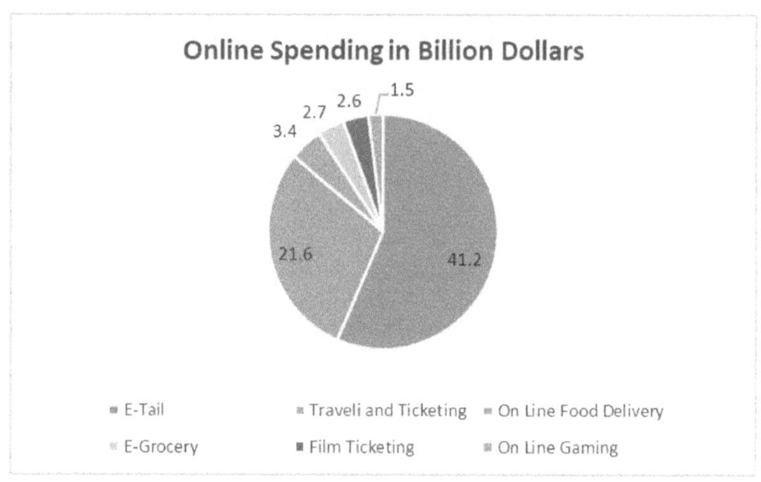

Source: California Life science Times of India*3

E-commerce Verticals and Marketplaces:

E-commerce platforms in India have diversified their offerings across various verticals, including electronics, fashion, groceries, and services. Marketplaces like Amazon and Flipkart have enabled small sellers and businesses to reach a wider audience and participate in the e-commerce ecosystem.

Logistics and Last-Mile Delivery:

Logistics infrastructure and last-mile delivery capabilities have emerged as critical factors in the success of e-commerce platforms. Companies have invested in building robust logistics networks, warehousing facilities, and delivery mechanisms to ensure timely and efficient fulfillment of orders.

Digital Payments and Cashless Transactions:

E-commerce has been a catalyst for the adoption of digital

payments and cashless transactions in India. Platforms have integrated various payment options, including credit/debit cards, net banking, mobile wallets, and UPI, to offer convenience and security to customers.

Regulatory Challenges and Policy Framework:

E-commerce in India has faced regulatory challenges related to foreign direct investment (FDI) regulations, competition policy, and taxation. The government has introduced guidelines and regulations to address these challenges, including FDI norms for e-commerce marketplaces and GST regulations for online transactions.

Rise of Reliance in the E-Commerce:

Mukesh Ambani-led Reliance is in the best position to tap the blooming Indian e-commerce sector. Reliance is currently number three with an estimated $5.7 billion in e-commerce sales driven by attractive categories of fashion (Ajio) and JioMart (E-grocery). As reported in "The Hindu Business Online" news, Reliance is building the largest digital ecosystem in India. Its Telecom arm, Jio, with 430 million mobile subscribers (and still growing!), and retail arm with 18, 300 retail stores, will support reliance on its digital dream. Its digital mix is scaling up 17-18 percent ($6 Billion, E-commerce business).

Open Network for Digital Commerce:

ONDC is an initiative of government of India to revolutionize the digital commerce ecosystem in the country. Through ONDC government aims to promote fair competition, enhance user convenience, and foster innovation. It was meant to break the stranglehold of e-commerce giants — Amazon, Flipkart, Zomato, Swiggy and their Peers.

The network has scaled up rapidly to clock 2.6 lakh orders per day. According to Mr. Koshy, the CEO of ONDC, it hit a peak of 2.87 lakh orders per day. Another aspect the network can boast of is that more than 60 percent of its orders are from tier-2 cities. Annual transactions for the Current financial year had touched 41.2 million by March 1.

Future Outlook and Opportunities:

ONDC is an initiative of government of India to revolutionize the digital commerce ecosystem in the country. Through ONDC government aims to promote fair competition, enhance user convenience, and foster innovation. it was meant to break the stranglehold of e-commerce giants — Amazon, Flipkart, Zomato, Swiggy and their Peers.

The network has scaled up rapidly to clock 2.6 lakh orders per day. According to Mr. Koshy, the CEO of ONDC, it hit a peak of 2.87 lakh orders per day. Another aspect the network can boast of is that more than 60 percent of its orders are from tier-

2 cities. Annual transactions for the Current financial year had touched 41.2 million by March 1.

Future Outlook and Opportunities:

The future of e-commerce in India is poised for continued growth and innovation, driven by increasing internet penetration, digital adoption, and changing consumer behaviour. Opportunities abound for e-commerce platforms to leverage emerging technologies such as AI, AR/VR, and blockchain to enhance customer experience, optimize operations, and expand into new markets and verticals.

The rise of e-commerce platforms in India represents a paradigm shift in the country's retail and commerce landscape, catalysing digital growth, empowerment, and innovation. As e-commerce evolves and matures, it will play an increasingly prominent role in shaping consumer behavior, market dynamics, and economic growth in India. Collaboration between stakeholders, regulatory clarity, and investments in technology and infrastructure will be crucial to realizing the full potential of e-commerce in India's digital growth story.

Resources:

1. https://www.businessapac.com/e-commerce-companies-in-india/
2. https://www.ibef.org/industry/ecommerce

3. https://www.mordorintelligence.com/industry-reports/india-ecommerce-market
4. https://economictimes.indiatimes.com/tech/technology/is-ondcs-gamble-paying-off/articleshow/108551666.cms?utm_source=contentof interest&utm_medium=text&utm_campaign=cpps

8. The Growth of Mobile Phone Usage and Smartphone Penetration in India

The mobile revolution has been a driving force behind India's digital growth story, transforming the way people communicate, access information, and engage with digital services. India is aiming to manufacture mobile phones worth $126 Bn by 2025-26*1.

Early Adoption of Mobile Phones:

The introduction of mobile telephony in India in the 1990s marked a significant milestone in the country's communication landscape. Early mobile phones were primarily used for voice calls and text messaging, providing basic connectivity to urban and semi-urban populations.

Expansion of Mobile Networks:

The liberalization of India's telecom sector in the 1990s led to the entry of private players and the expansion of mobile networks across the country. Initiatives such as the National Telecom Policy and the auction of spectrum licenses fueled competition and investment in telecom infrastructure.

Rise of Feature Phones:

Feature phones emerged as the dominant mobile device in India during the early 2000s, offering affordable and basic communication capabilities to a mass audience. Companies like

Nokia, Samsung, and Micromax captured the market with a wide range of feature phone models catering to diverse consumer needs.

Smartphone Revolution:

The advent of smartphones revolutionized the mobile landscape in India and offered advanced computing capabilities.

It helped in social connectivity and access to a wide range of digital services.

The launch of affordable smartphones by companies like, Reliance Jio, Xiaomi, Realme, and Vivo democratized access to technology, driving smartphone penetration across socio-economic segments. India added over 500 million new smartphone users in the last 10 years. Business analysts expect 850 million smartphone users by 2026, representing ~55% of the total population[1].

According to another survey by Satista the number of smartphone users in India was estimated to reach over one billion in 2024. It is estimated that by 2030, the number of smartphone users in India will reach 1.35 billion.

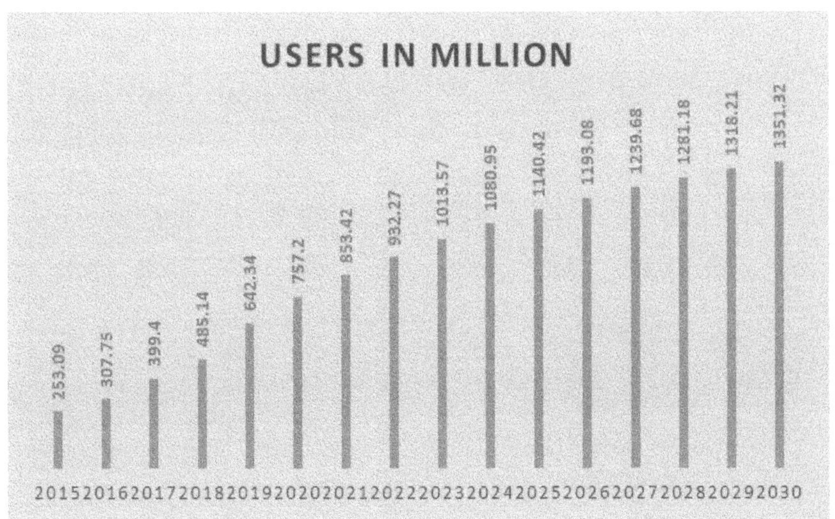

Source* 2.

Contradicting above predictions India's smartphone market shipped 146 million smartphones in 2023, with a nominal 1% growth YoY (year-over-year). Consumer demand remained stressed, which led to excess inventory levels across the country despite price corrections and different attractive schemes by vendors. Analysts attributed the shipment decline to inflationary pressure, component shortage, and the Russia-Ukraine war. The table below shows the Top 10 mobile brands with YOY growth.

- Apple had a good growth finishing at 9 million units. This was led by previous generation iPhone models and its push for local manufacturing. Its iPhone 13/14 were among the Top 5 shipped models annually.

- Samsung saw negative growth of 5% but remained in the leadership position, with a record high ASP of US$338. Its Galaxy A14 was the highest-shipped device of 2023.

- vivo (excluding iQOO) climbed to the second slot as shipments and ASPs both grew by 8% and 9%, respectively.

- Realme, despite facing challenges in the beginning of the year, maintained its third position, led by affordable launches.

Brands	2022 Market Share	2023 Market Share	Year-over-Year unit change
1. Samsung	18.1%	17.0%	-5.3%
2. Vivo	14.1%	15.2%	8.2%
3. Realme	14.5%	12.5%	-12.9%
4. Xiaomi	17.8%	12.4%	-29.6%
5. OPPO	11.9%	10.3%	-12.2%
6. Apple	4.6%	6.4%	38.6%
7. OnePlus	4.1%	6.1%	48.7%
8. Poco	3.2%	4.9%	54.2%
9. Infinix	2.3%	3.1%	39.8%
10. Tecno	2.4%	2.9%	19.9%
Others	7.0%	9.2%	33.0%
Total	100.0%	100.0%	0.8%

Source *3

The market share of India's Top 5 mobile brand companies is illustrated in the image below. With over 20% of the market share, Xiaomi is leading in India, followed by Samsung with 18.17%. Samsung and Realme are close third and fourth. Oppo, with 11.52% of the market, has taken fifth position. In India,

Apple holds just 3.35% of the market share.

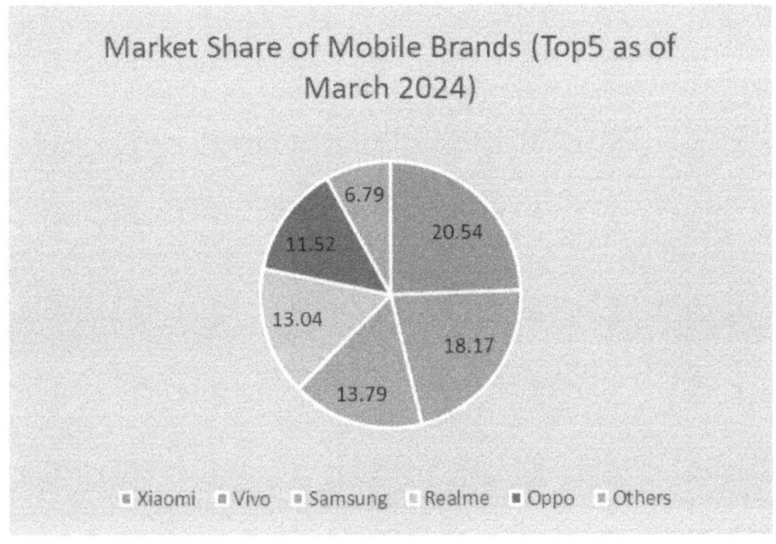

Source *4

Factors Driving Smartphone Adoption:

Several factors contributed to the rapid adoption of smartphones in India, including declining device prices, increasing disposable incomes, and improving internet infrastructure. The availability of affordable data plans and the launch of 4G networks further accelerated smartphone adoption, fuelling demand for data-intensive applications and services.

Impact on Digital Access and Inclusion:

The widespread adoption of smartphones has democratized access to information, education, and digital services, particularly in rural and underserved areas. Mobile internet penetration has enabled millions of Indians to access government services, e-commerce platforms, educational content, and financial services through smartphones.

Role in Economic Growth and Innovation:

The mobile revolution has fuelled economic growth and innovation in India, catalyzing the development of e-commerce, fintech, and digital media industries. Mobile-first approaches have enabled startups and businesses to reach a wider audience, innovate new products and services, and drive entrepreneurship and job creation.

Outlook and Challenges:

The future of mobile technology in India looks promising, with increasing smartphone penetration and the advent of 5G networks expected to unlock new opportunities for innovation and economic growth. However, challenges such as digital divide, cybersecurity threats, and privacy concerns must be addressed to ensure equitable access to mobile technology and safeguard user rights in the digital age.

With increasing smartphone penetration and evolving mobile technologies, India is poised to leverage mobile technology as a catalyst for socio-economic development and digital empowerment in the years to come. Collaboration between government, industry, and other stakeholders will be essential in addressing challenges and harnessing the full potential of the mobile revolution to realize India's vision of a digitally empowered nation.

Resources:

1. https://www.investindia.gov.in/sector/telecom
2. https://www.statista.com/statistics/467163/forecast-of-smartphone-users-in-india/
3. https://www.idc.com/getdoc.jsp?containerId=prAP51865624
4. https://gs.statcounter.com/vendor-market-share/mobile/india

9. Digital Payments: Empowering Financial Inclusion in India's Digital Growth Story

Digital payments have emerged as a cornerstone of India's digital growth story, revolutionizing how transactions are conducted and driving financial inclusion across the country.

Early Initiatives and Challenges:

The concept of digital payments in India dates back to the introduction of electronic funds transfer (EFT) systems in the 1980s. However, adopting digital payments faced significant challenges, including low banking penetration, lack of internet connectivity, and consumer apprehension towards online transactions.

Regulatory Framework and Policy Interventions:

The Reserve Bank of India (RBI) played a pivotal role in laying the regulatory framework for digital payments in India. Initiatives like the Payment and Settlement Systems Act, 2007, and the National Payments Corporation of India (NPCI) were introduced to regulate and streamline digital payment systems in the country.

Rising Adoption of Digital Payments:

India has experienced a surge in digital payments adoption, driven by increasing smartphone penetration, internet connectivity, and government initiatives. Mobile wallets, UPI, and digital payment platforms have emerged as preferred transaction modes for consumers, merchants, and businesses. The graph below from Statista shows an exponential increase YOY in digital payment. Digital payment increased from 14.59 billion in 2018 to 113.95 billion in 2023. At the same time, payments in FY2020, FY2021, and FY2022 can be attributed to COVID-19; growth in 2023 shows that digital payment is increasing.

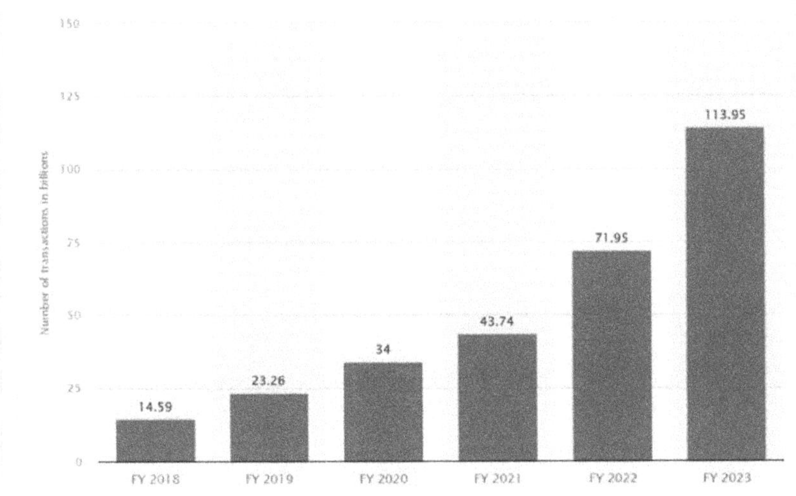

Total number of digital payments across India from financial year 2018 to 2023(in billions) Source*1

Revolutionizing Payments with UPI:

When it was launched in 2016, the Unified Payments Interface (UPI) revolutionized the digital payments landscape in India. UPI enabled seamless, real-time payments directly from bank accounts, bypassing the need for traditional payment instruments such as credit/debit cards and net banking.

UPI is making a remarkable contribution to India's economic development by promoting financial inclusion. Undoubtedly, demonetization made a big push for digital payment and UPI usage. During Covid-19, as people chose to maintain their social distance, cashless digital payments got major praise. As per the Economic Survey Report 2023, the Indian economy saw digital transactions through UPI worth Rs. 126 lakh crores in 2022.

The graph below exhibits the highlights of the UPI journey in India, with YoY (Year-on-Year) growth statistics until January 2023, from its inception in 2016.

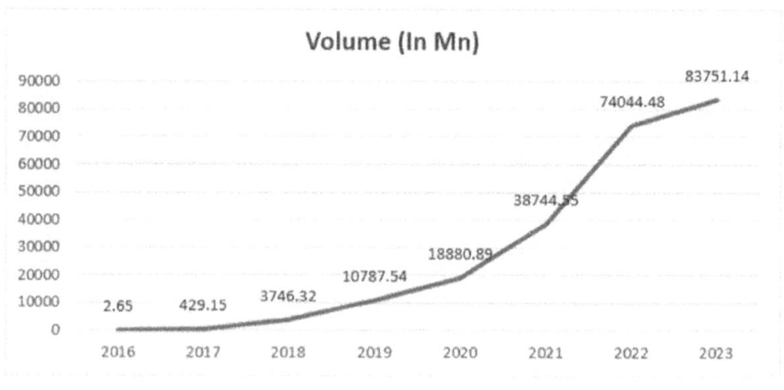

Source*2

The above statistics showcase the increasing popularity of UPI in India. The steep jump from 3756Mn in 2018 to 74044n in 2022 due to demonetization and the impact of COVID-19.

Today, UPI usage is not just limited to India; many countries are now adopting this cashless payment method worldwide.

The table below list the lists the countries that are accepting the UPI payment.

India	Singapore	South Korea
Armenia	Thailand	Bahrain
Bhutan	Cambodia	Maldives
Nepal	Vietnam	United Arab Emirates
France	Sri Lanka	Australia
Qatar	Indonesia	Japan
Saudi Arabia	Oman	Switzerland
Malaysia	Mauritius	Canada
United Kingdom	European Union	Russia

Source*3 (Times of India)

In addition, the National Payments Corporation of India (NPCI) is discussing with many countries, including the USA, the European Union, and other West Asian countries, to extend UPI services to their countries.

For smaller value transactions, UPI Lite has become popular. It enables UPI users to transfer up to ₹200 in just a single click. No pin is needed, and a ticket-sized UPI transaction can be quickly made. Reserve Bank of India has recently increased the transaction limit to ₹500. Now, every month, more than 10 million transactions are processed through UPI Lite*3.

Earlier, Paytm was the leading player, but Phone Pay and Google Pay are taking its place. The table below shows the share of UPI apps in all UPI transactions.

UPI APPs	Market Share
Phone Pay	46%
Google Pay	36%
Paytm	13%
Others	5%

PhonePe is the leading player in the UPI market, with 46% of the share. Google Pay and Paytm remained second and third players in India's UPI payments market.

UPI continue to gain popularity and become the preferred mode of payment, but the biggest concern is rising fraud incidences. More than 95,4020 UPI fraud cases were reported in the financial year 2023, and the number of reported cases increased after COVID-19. Impersonating sellers, OTP and PIN fraud, Phishing, and malware are some of the examples of common UPI frauds.

FASTag:

FASTag uses RFID (Radio Frequency Identification Technology) technology to make the payment at the Toll while the vehicle is in motion. It was developed by the National Payment Corporation of India (NPCI) to meet the new-age Indian market requirements. FASTag offers the convenience of cashless payment, and in addition, one can save on fuel and time as the customer does not have to stop at the toll plaza.

FASTag provides an interoperable, secure framework capable of use across the country. FASTag issued by any registered member bank is accepted at all toll plazas. Since all transactions are carried out digitally, they increase transparency and make auditing easy. Customers can recharge their FASTag account online through the member bank's portal using UPI/ Credit Card/ Debit Card/ NEFT/ RTGS /Net Banking.

The Chart below shows the volume of transactions and amounts collected from 2016 to 2024. In 2022-23, more than 541 billion rupees were collected.

Year-wise growth in FASTag

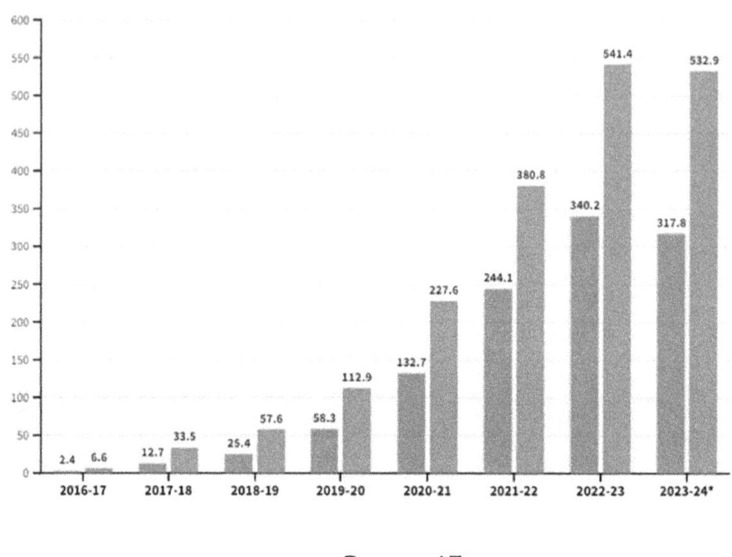

Source*5

FasTag has increased toll collection for the government; it is estimated that an average of 29% more tax is collected compared to the manual toll system. This collected money can be used for further development of highways and infrastructure. As per the Standing Committee on Transport, Tourism, and Culture, FASTag has saved approximately 463 million hours of vehicle time, which is equivalent to Rs 34000 crores of economic value. By using FasTag, waiting time for vehicles at the toll gate is substantially reduced.

Now, the government is going one step ahead; as per highway minister Mr. Gadkari, FASTag will be replaced with a GPS-based toll collection system to eliminate Toll plazas. This new system is expected to smooth highway traffic and help in faster journeys.

Mobile Wallets and Digital Payment Platforms:

The proliferation of mobile wallets such as Paytm, PhonePe, and Google Pay significantly drove digital payments adoption in India. These platforms offered convenience, security, and cashback incentives, attracting a large user base, and facilitating a shift towards cashless transactions.

Aadhaar-enabled Payments:

The Aadhaar biometric identification system facilitated the adoption of Aadhaar-enabled payment systems (AEPS), enabling secure and convenient transactions using biometric authentication. AEPS played a crucial role in promoting financial inclusion by providing banking services to unbanked and underbanked populations in rural areas.

Government Initiatives and Incentives:

The Indian government introduced various initiatives and incentives to promote digital payment adoption and drive financial inclusion. Programs such as Digital India, Jan Dhan Yojana, and Pradhan Mantri Mudra Yojana aimed to expand access to banking services, promote cashless transactions and empower individuals with digital financial literacy.

Expansion of Digital Payments Ecosystem:

The digital payments ecosystem in India has expanded beyond urban centers to rural and semi-urban areas, driven by initiatives such as Jan Dhan Yojana and Aadhaar-enabled payments. Government programs and incentives have played a crucial role in promoting financial inclusion and driving digital payment adoption among underserved populations.

Emerging Trends in Digital Payments:

Emerging technologies such as blockchain, artificial intelligence (AI), and machine learning (ML) are transforming the digital payments landscape, enabling enhanced security, efficiency, and personalization. Subscription-based payments, peer-to-peer lending, and embedded finance are among the emerging trends reshaping the future of digital payments in India.

Challenges and Opportunities:

Despite the significant progress in digital payments adoption, India continues to face challenges such as cybersecurity threats, interoperability issues, and last-mile connectivity challenges. Cybersecurity threats such as phishing attacks, malware, and data breaches pose risks to consumer data and financial stability, necessitating robust security measures and awareness campaigns.

However, these challenges also present opportunities for

innovation and collaboration, particularly in leveraging emerging technologies such as blockchain and AI to address these issues.

Future Outlook and Conclusion:

The future of digital payments in India is promising, with continued growth expected in both urban and rural areas. As India embraces digital payments as a mainstream mode of transaction, it is poised to realize the vision of a less-cash economy, driving economic growth, financial inclusion, and empowerment for millions of Indians.

Digital payments have emerged as a transformative force in India's digital growth story, driving financial inclusion, economic empowerment, and innovation. As the country continues its journey towards a cashless economy, collaboration between stakeholders, regulatory clarity, and investments in technology and infrastructure will be crucial to realizing the full potential of digital payments in India.

Resources:
1.   https://www.statista.com/statistics/1251321/india-total-volume-of-digital-payments/

2.   https://www.nic.in/blogs/digital-payments-driving-the-growth-of-digital-economy/

3. https://www.cashfree.com/blog/upi-transaction-limit/

4. https://www.demandsage.com/upi-statistics/

5. https://factly.in/data-fastag-collections-cross-rs-50000-crores-in-2022-23-and-even-in-2023-24/

10. Driving Digital Growth: Technological Innovations and Start-ups Shaping India's Digital Landscape

Technological innovations have driven India's digital growth story, revolutionizing industries, transforming governance, and empowering individuals.

Aadhaar, India's biometric identification system, has played a pivotal role in enabling secure and convenient access to government services and financial transactions. Aadhaar authentication has streamlined processes such as identity verification, KYC (Know Your Customer), and subsidy distribution, driving efficiency and transparency in governance and financial services.

Artificial Intelligence (AI) and Machine Learning (ML):

AI and ML technologies are transforming healthcare, finance, agriculture, and manufacturing industries. Applications of AI and ML include predictive analytics, personalized recommendations, fraud detection, and process automation, driving efficiency, innovation, and competitiveness in businesses and organizations.

AI can be integrated into the digital economy, streamlining business processes to prepare personalized solutions. AI, data-driven approaches, generative AI, and the Internet of Things will boost the digital economy. Banks and financial associates, with the help of AI and RPA (Robotic Process Automation), can free up critical resources, effectively reducing operation costs without compromising quality and time schedule*1.

Internet of Things (IoT) and Smart Infrastructure:

The Internet of Things (IoT) is revolutionizing infrastructure and urban services, enabling the development of smart cities and intelligent transportation systems. IoT applications include smart meters, connected vehicles, remote monitoring systems, and environmental sensors, enhancing efficiency, sustainability, and quality of life in urban areas. IoT collects a large volume of data.

AI is used for Data analysis. It recognizes different patterns and makes decisions based on the analysis.

IoT is now used in India for many applications such as smart homes, smart cities, agriculture, environment monitoring, water management, disaster management, health monitoring, and hospital management systems*2.

As per Statista, the IoT market in India is expected to grow substantially for the next few years. From 2024 to 2028, the IoT market is expected to grow at a rate of 17.05% annually. Analysis expects that by 2028, IoT market volume will reach ₹5,036.00 billion*3.

Blockchain Technology and Digital Trust:

Blockchain technology can potentially revolutionize digital trust, security, and transparency in various sectors such as finance, supply chain, and governance. Blockchain applications include cryptocurrency, smart contracts, supply chain tracking, and identity management, fostering trust, accountability, and decentralization in digital transactions and interactions.

As per the strategy published by The Ministry of Electronics and IT on the blockchain, the Indian government plans to implement blockchain technology in finance, e-governance, healthcare, smart cities, and other domains. The government has also announced a five-year plan, the National Blockchain Framework, to implement blockchain in diverse industries[7]. According to the Economic Times, the Blockchain market in India is expected to record a CAGR of 47.3% and reach $4.3 billion by 2025[8].

Renewable Energy and Sustainable Technologies:

India is embracing renewable energy and sustainable technologies to address environmental challenges and meet growing energy demands. Innovations in solar energy, wind power, energy storage, and green technologies are driving the transition towards a cleaner, more sustainable energy future, reducing carbon emissions and dependence on fossil fuels.

Emerging Technologies and Future Outlook:

Emerging technologies such as 5G, quantum computing, augmented reality (AR), and virtual reality (VR) hold immense potential to accelerate India's digital growth trajectory further. These technologies are expected to revolutionize industries, create new business opportunities, and reshape how people live, work, and interact in the digital age.

The Emergence of India's Startup Ecosystem:

India's startup ecosystem has emerged as a vibrant and dynamic force driving innovation, entrepreneurship, and economic growth in the country. The Indian government recognized the importance of startups as engines of innovation and job creation, launching initiatives such as Startup India to support the growth of the ecosystem. Policy reforms such as simplification of regulations, tax incentives, and easier access to funding have been introduced to create a conducive environment for startups to thrive.

India has witnessed the rise of several unicorns - startups valued at over $1 billion - across various sectors, including e-commerce, fintech, edtech, and healthcare. Companies like Flipkart, Paytm, Ola, and BYJU'S have become household names, attracting significant investments and reshaping industries with their disruptive business models.

In January 2016 the Indian government started an initiative

called "Startup India," a flagship project with the vision of catalyzing the start-up culture and building a strong and inclusive ecosystem for innovation and entrepreneurship in India. This initiative helped in shaping the start-up ecosystem and business thrive*4.

The government announces many schemes for start-ups : 1. Atal innovation mission (AIM) 2. Start-up India seed fund scheme 3. Start-up India Initiative 4. Aatmanirbhar Bharat App Innovation Challenge etc.. which are helping for economic progress and innovation*5.

As per the government reports, India is the 3rd largest ecosystem for start-ups globally with over 1,12,718 recognized start-ups across the country as of October 2023. Indian Start-up Ecosystem has seen exponential growth in past 10 years. There is 15X growth in the start-up funding, 9X increase in the number of investors, and 7X increase in the number of incubators. Now India is home to Approximately 111 unicorns with a total valuation of $349.67 Billion. Today, 1 out every 10 unicorns globally have been born in India*6.

Startups in India are not just replicating successful models from the West but are innovating to address local challenges and cater to unique market needs. Sectors such as agri-tech, health-tech, cleantech, and deep-tech are witnessing a surge in startup activity, driven by technological advancements and a growing focus on social impact.

The future of India's startup ecosystem looks promising, with a growing number of startups poised to scale globally and significantly impact the world stage. Collaborations with international partners, access to global markets, and a supportive policy environment will be essential in realizing the full potential of India's startups as engines of innovation and economic prosperity.

Technological innovations have driven India's digital growth story, empowering individuals, transforming industries, and reshaping society. From mobile technology and digital payments to AI, IoT, and blockchain, these innovations are revolutionizing various sectors and fuelling economic growth, innovation, and development. As India continues its journey towards digital transformation, embracing emerging technologies and fostering innovation will be essential to realizing the full potential of the digital revolution and building a more inclusive, sustainable, and prosperous future for all. India's startups are poised to make a significant impact on the global stage, driving positive change and shaping the future of industries across the world.

Resources:
1. https://indiaai.gov.in/article/the-role-of-ai-in-shaping-india-s-digital-economy

2. https://www.iotforall.com/the-impact-of-iot-and-digital-transformation-on-india

3. https://www.researchgate.net/publication/376313943_Unleashing_the_IoT_Revolution_in_India_Trends_Advantages_Applications_and_Strategic_Importance

4. https://www.linkedin.com/pulse/growth-story-indian-startup-ecosystem-ticenews-z9nac/

5. https://timesofindia.indiatimes.com/blogs/truth-lies-and-politics/contribution-startups-revolution-is-making-to-indias-growth/

6. https://www.investindia.gov.in/indian-unicorn-landscape

7. https://www.bennett.edu.in/media-center/blog/what-is-the-government-of-indias-stand-on-blockchain-applications-in-diverse-industries/#:~:text=The%20Government%20of%20India%20is%20implementing%20blockchain%20technology%20in%20diverse,and%20proof%2Dof%2Dexistence.

8. https://economictimes.indiatimes.com/tech/technology/indian-web3-industry-to-reach-1-1-billion-by-2032-report/articleshow/98632635.cms?from=mdr

11.   Challenges in India's Digital Growth Path

While India's digital growth story has been remarkable, it has not been without its share of challenges. Regulatory hurdles and policy bottlenecks have often hindered the pace of innovation and growth in the country's digital ecosystem.

Complex Regulatory Environment:

India's regulatory landscape is often characterized by complexity, ambiguity, and inconsistency across different sectors and jurisdictions. Businesses operating in fintech, e-commerce, and telecommunications face regulatory challenges related to licensing, compliance, taxation, and data privacy.

Foreign Direct Investment (FDI) Regulations:

FDI regulations in sectors such as e-commerce and digital media have been subject to frequent changes and controversies, leading to uncertainty among investors and businesses. Policy changes such as restrictions on FDI in e-commerce marketplaces and digital media platforms have impacted business models and market dynamics, necessitating adaptations and compliance measures.

Data Privacy and Protection:

Data privacy and protection have emerged as key regulatory concerns in India, particularly in light of increasing digital transactions, data breaches, and privacy violations. The absence of comprehensive data protection legislation and ambiguity surrounding data localization requirements pose challenges for businesses in terms of compliance, risk management, and customer trust. To address the data protection issues, the government of India passed the Digital Personal Data Protection (DPDP) Act, 2023, but its effectiveness is still to be tested.

Cybersecurity Regulations:

Cybersecurity threats pose significant risks to businesses, government entities, and consumers in India, necessitating robust regulatory frameworks and proactive measures to mitigate risks. While initiatives such as the National Cyber Security Policy and CERT-In aim to enhance cybersecurity preparedness, challenges remain in terms of enforcement, coordination, and capacity building.

Taxation and Regulatory Compliance:

Taxation policies and regulatory compliance requirements in India can be complex and burdensome for businesses, particularly startups and small enterprises. Issues such as multiple taxation regimes, indirect taxes, and compliance costs can deter investment, innovation, and entrepreneurship, stifling growth and competitiveness.

Intellectual Property Rights (IPR) Protection:

Intellectual property rights (IPR) protection is essential for fostering innovation, creativity, and competitiveness in the digital economy. Challenges such as lengthy registration processes, backlog of patent applications, and enforcement issues undermine the effectiveness of IPR protection in India, impacting investment and innovation.

Regulatory Arbitrage and Policy Uncertainty:

Regulatory arbitrage, where businesses exploit regulatory loopholes or inconsistencies to gain competitive advantage, is a common phenomenon in India's digital ecosystem. Policy uncertainty, frequent changes in regulations, and lack of clarity on regulatory intent create challenges for businesses in terms of planning, investment, and risk management.

Collaboration and Stakeholder Engagement:

Addressing regulatory hurdles and policy bottlenecks requires collaboration and stakeholder engagement among government, industry, civil society, and other stakeholders. Dialogue, transparency, and consultation mechanisms can facilitate better understanding, alignment of interests, and co-creation of regulatory frameworks that balance innovation, consumer protection, and public interest.

Regulatory hurdles and policy bottlenecks pose significant challenges to India's digital growth story, impacting innovation, investment, and competitiveness in the digital ecosystem. Addressing these challenges requires the efforts from government, industry, and other stakeholders to create clear, consistent, and enabling regulatory frameworks that foster innovation, protect consumer interests, and promote economic growth. By addressing regulatory challenges and embracing a culture of innovation and collaboration, India can unlock the full potential of its digital economy and realize its vision of a digitally empowered and inclusive nation.

12.   Strategies for Sustaining and Accelerating Digital Growth in India

Despite the challenges and hurdles, India's digital landscape presents numerous opportunities for further growth and development.

Hyperconnected Society:

By 2030, India will become a hyperconnected society, with ubiquitous access to high-speed internet, smart devices, and digital services across urban and rural areas. The proliferation of 5G networks, satellite internet, and next-generation connectivity solutions will ensure seamless connectivity, enabling all citizens' real-time communication, collaboration, and access to information.

Rural and Underserved Market Expansion:

One of the most significant opportunities lies in expanding digital services and solutions to rural and underserved markets. With increasing internet penetration and smartphone adoption in rural areas, there is a vast untapped market for e-commerce, fintech, healthtech, and edtech solutions tailored to the needs of rural communities.

Digital Literacy and Skill Development:

Investing in digital literacy and skill development initiatives presents an opportunity to empower individuals with the knowledge and skills needed to participate in the digital economy. Programs focused on digital literacy, coding, data science, and emerging technologies can bridge the digital divide and unlock the potential of India's youth as creators, innovators, and entrepreneurs.

To ensure quality education and skill development to all Indians, government has launched the skill India program. The vision of this platform is to provide relevant skill and courses for better job opportunities and entrepreneurship support. Platform work under the framework to build the Digital Public Infrastructure and the digital economy. Program wants to ensure people from diverse backgrounds to access the platform easily, regardless of the technology they had.

Innovation in Emerging Technologies:

India has the talent, expertise, and ecosystem to become a global hub for innovation in emerging technologies such as artificial intelligence (AI), blockchain, the Internet of Things (IoT), and augmented reality (AR)/virtual reality (VR).

Leveraging these technologies across sectors such as healthcare, agriculture, manufacturing, and smart cities can drive efficiency, productivity, and competitiveness, opening up new opportunities for growth and development.

Digital Health and Telemedicine:

The COVID-19 pandemic has accelerated the adoption of

digital health solutions, creating opportunities for telemedicine, remote monitoring, and digital healthcare delivery. Investing in digital health infrastructure, interoperable systems, and telemedicine platforms can improve access to quality healthcare, reduce healthcare costs, and enhance healthcare outcomes for millions of Indians.

Smart Cities and Urban Development:

India's urbanization presents opportunities for leveraging technology and digital solutions to address urban challenges and promote sustainable development. Smart city initiatives focused on digital infrastructure, mobility solutions, energy efficiency, and citizen services can enhance quality of life, promote economic growth, and create vibrant, liveable cities.

Digital Financial Inclusion:

Promoting digital financial inclusion presents an opportunity to bring millions of unbanked and underbanked individuals into the formal financial system. Innovations in digital payments, microfinance, and digital banking services can improve access to financial services, enable savings, credit, and insurance, and empower individuals with financial resilience and security.

Industry 4.0 and Digital Manufacturing:

India's manufacturing sector has the potential to leapfrog into the era of Industry 4.0 by embracing digital technologies such as automation, robotics, and predictive analytics. Digitizing manufacturing processes, supply chains, and operations can enhance productivity, quality, and agility, making Indian industries competitive and driving economic growth globally.

Green Technology and Sustainability:

India has a growing opportunity to lead the transition towards green technology and sustainable development. Investments in renewable energy, clean transportation, waste management, and sustainable agriculture can address environmental challenges, create green jobs, and promote inclusive and resilient growth.

Fostering Innovation Ecosystems:

Streamline regulations, reduce bureaucratic hurdles, and provide incentives for startups and SMEs to create a conducive environment for innovation and entrepreneurship. Establish innovation hubs, technology parks, and incubation centers to nurture talent, foster collaboration, and support the development of innovative solutions across sectors.

Encouraging Investment and Funding:

Encourage domestic and foreign investment in India's digital ecosystem by offering incentives, tax breaks, and regulatory certainty for investors and businesses. Facilitate access to funding through venture capital, angel investors, and public-private partnerships to support the growth of startups and innovative ventures.

Strengthening Cybersecurity and Data Protection:

Enhance cybersecurity infrastructure, capabilities, and awareness to mitigate cyber threats, protect critical infrastructure, and safeguard digital assets. Implement robust data protection regulations and mechanisms to ensure the privacy, security, and integrity of personal and sensitive data in accordance with international standards.

Leveraging Emerging Technologies:

Embrace emerging technologies such as artificial intelligence (AI), blockchain, the Internet of Things (IoT), and edge computing to drive innovation, efficiency, and competitiveness across sectors. Foster collaboration between industry, academia, and research institutions to explore applications and use cases for emerging technologies in healthcare, agriculture, manufacturing, and smart cities.

Engaging in Global Partnerships and Collaboration:

Strengthen international collaborations and partnerships to share best practices, knowledge, and resources for advancing digital growth and development. Participate in global forums, initiatives, and standards-setting bodies to shape the global digital agenda and contribute to collective efforts towards achieving sustainable and inclusive digital transformation.

I would like to conclude with Nanadan Nilekani Sir's thoughts on India's Digital transformation and Digital India which are very relevant, inspirational, and insightful. India has witnessed tremendous growth in the last 10 years, which otherwise would have taken four to five decades. When we discuss the future of India and its ambitions, it is important to understand what non-linear changes have happened, what non-linear changes will happen, and its impacts on further changes leading to the combinatorial Innovation phenomenon. All these changes are interacting with each other and creating new opportunities and threats, which need to be addressed. India is going through a massive upgrade from a cash, informal, low-productivity economy to an online, cashless, formal, High-productive economy. This may not happen in one year or two years. It may take ten years or 15 years, but the fundamental building blocks are in place, the fundamental momentum is in place, and we need to think about how to leverage and take advantage of this massive transition, which is one of a kind and happens only once in the history of a country.